THE LITTLE
MARMALADE
Cat Book

DAVID TAYLOR
ELIZABETH MARTYN

DORLING KINDERSLEY ◆ LONDON

DORLING KINDERSLEY ◆ LONDON

PROJECT EDITOR *Corinne Hall*

PROJECT ART EDITOR *Nigel Hazle*

MANAGING ART EDITOR *Nick Harris*

MANAGING EDITOR *Vicky Davenport*

*First published in Great Britain in 1990 by
Dorling Kindersley Limited 9 Henrietta Street London WC2E 8PS
Reprinted 1990*

British Library Cataloguing in Publication Data

The little marmalade cat book.
1. Pets: cats
I. Title II. Series
636.8
ISBN 0-83618-453-7

Printed and bound in Italy by Mondadori.

CONTENTS

CREATIVE
Cats

The marmalade cat as inspiration in the art, literature and mythology of all ages, the whole world over.

FANTASY AND FOLKLORE

Marmalade cats have featured in fantasy and folklore for thousands of years. Here are some fascinating examples.

The Scots are traditionally fond of cats and thought that to have one in the home guaranteed happiness. A new feline arrival would have its paws rubbed briskly on the chimneypiece to ensure that it never ran away, taking happiness with it.

PRACTICAL JOKER

A marmalade cat renowned for his disappearing tricks is Macavity, from T. S. Eliot's *Old Possum's Book of Practical Cats*. Master criminal, he is also disconcertingly humanoid!

MARVELLOUS MARMALADES

Marmalade cats are popular heroes in children's books. The best-known may be Kathleen Hale's Orlando, who has delighted several generations of children.

In "The Baker's Cat" by Joan Aiken, a huge marmalade cat, Mog, eats some of the baker's yeast and swells to an enormous size - big enough, fortunately, to save the village from flood by blocking the path of the waters when a nearby river breaks its banks. A more sinister marmalade cat, Ginger, features in C. S. Lewis's classic *The Last Battle*, from the loved and much-read Narnia chronicles. Ginger is in collusion with the evil forces that threaten to overtake the entire country, but gets his come-uppance when he is transformed from talking beast back into dumb animal by the god Tash.

Far Left:
Youthful
Marmalade-Cat
Acrobats;
Below Left:
Magnificent
Marmalade Cat;
Left:
Lewis Carroll's
Grinning Ginger
Cat

SAY "CHEESE"

A cat who came and went exactly as he pleased was Lewis Carroll's enigmatic, smiling Cheshire Cat.

In his much-loved and much-read story book *Alice's Adventures in Wonderland*, the mysterious and mesmerising marmalade cat made Alice completely giddy by vanishing and leaving nothing but a disembodied, toothy grin suspended in the air. There is much speculation as to why this cat was so curiously named. A possible explanation is that whole, round Cheshire cheeses were traditionally stamped with a grinning cat's face, or even moulded in the shape of a cat.

Amazing Marmalade-Cat Facts

Cats are fascinating to nearly everyone. Here are some tantalizing marmalade-cat facts to whet the appetite.

Known in Britain since medieval times, marmalade cats are less common than black and tabby cats. They come into their own in the Orient, Turkey and North Africa, where they exist in large numbers. A small handful of marmalade cats is also found in the western isles of Scotland, where they are perhaps a reminder of Viking occupation.

Marmalade Mixer

A case of mistaken identity brought Marmaduke Gingerbits, a particularly striking marmalade cat, to public prominence. His owners had returned from a summer holiday and couldn't find him anywhere. They concluded that he had been stolen and accused a neighbour of the deed.

A ferocious and long-drawn-out court battle ensued, at a cost of over £7,000, to decide who actually was the handsome cat's true owner.

FAT CAT

No one would have any trouble recognizing Mis, a Danish cat once named the fattest of cats in Europe. Weighing in at a hefty fifteen kilogrammes, Mis is taken for walks on a lead and otherwise spends most of his time between meals fast asleep. Cats do, however, have the ability to live for many days without food and with very little water. Their natural reaction is not to panic when trapped. This way they manage to conserve energy by remaining completely calm and quiet.

Left: A Rather Superior Marmalade Cat; Right: The Ultimate Conservatory Cat; Below right: Sporting Marmalade Cat.

TIN RIBS

One cat who put this theory to the test was a ginger tom named Timmy. Exploring a building site, he crept into a hole in the wall to take a quiet nap. Builders bricked up the hole not knowing Timmy was inside, and he remained trapped for twenty-four days until a passing bricklayer heard his panic-stricken mews. It took the local police and fire brigade to dismantle the wall, to find Timmy thinner but otherwise unharmed by his adventure.

HALL OF FELINE FAME

Here are some marmalade cats that have graced the corridors of feline fame in literature, film and advertising.

A marmalade cat is a guaranteed scene-stealer in any film. Rhubarb, the cat who inherited a baseball team, was a marmalade street cat made good who ended up leading his team to fame and fortune. In *The Three Lives of Thomasina*, based on a novel by Paul Galico, the loss of a dearly beloved marmalade cat puts a child's life in grave danger.

LAZY BONES

A famously lazy marmalade cartoon cat is Garfield, whose character is best summed up in one of his favourite and most well-known sayings: "I'm fat, lazy and proud of it." This unscrupulous but still extremely likeable character's antics have been syndicated in newspapers all over the world.

A marmalade cat that was privy to the most sensitive of state secrets was Jock, Sir Winston Churchill's cat, who often sat in on Cabinet war meetings. Jock ate his meals with Churchill, who would send out his servants to look for the cat if ever he was missing at prime-ministerial meal times.

MARMALADE MAGNETISM

Morris, a marmalade cat who made his lucrative name in advertising, won a PATSY (Picture Animal Top Star of the Year) Award for his performance in a series of commercials for the American cat food Nine Lives. His fabulous, dignified features are loved, prized and instantly recognized the whole world over.

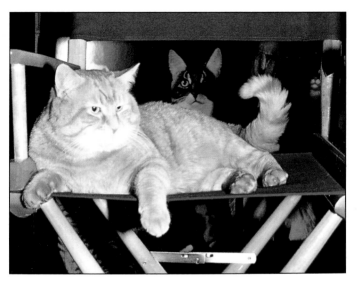

Left: Model Marmalade Cat;
Above: Marvellous Marmalade
Morris; Right: Companion Cat.

BREAKFAST MARMALADE

Cat is the somewhat unoriginal
name of the stunning ginger tom
who, in *Breakfast At Tiffany's*,
has the extreme good fortune
of playing opposite Audrey
Hepburn, but ends up being
kicked unceremoniously out of
her life when the going gets tough.

GALLERY OF
Cats

A sumptuous and select portrait gallery of marmalade cats - from luscious pedigree longhair to friendly family cat.

FELINE FEATURES

Every cat's features are uniquely expressive of its innermost character. Breeding often shows itself most obviously in the face, and especially in the eyes, the windows of the soul, which are also monitors of the slightest changes in mood, health or well-being. An alert, sparkling, interested cat is a joy to behold, as any cat lover will agree.

APRICOT
Red Tabby-point Siamese

TWINKLE
Red Classic Shorthair

CHLOE
British Cream Shorthair

MARMADUKE
Red Self Longhair

WILBUR
Non-pedigree

CLIVE
Non-pedigree

HORACE
Non-pedigree

TIZER
Non-pedigree

ARISTOCRATS
BRITISH CREAM SHORTHAIR

The paler the better is the rule for this head-turning cat. Its coat should be of the purest, palest cream without a hint of white and with only the faintest suspicion of any markings. For a long time no one knew the secret of breeding the British Cream, which occasionally cropped up among a brood of tortoiseshell kittens. Now they are bred from Creams or Blues, since tortoiseshells produce a coat with too deep a tinge of ginger. Getting the colour exactly right is complex, therefore perfection is difficult to come by.

*L*ATE RECOGNITION
The breed was first recognized in the 1920s, but didn't gain the greater popularity it now basks in for another thirty years or more.

Weather Vane
The British Cream's discreet
tabby markings sometimes
become more pronounced in
extremes of temperature.

Cateristics
🐈
That amazing fur is a delight
to cuddle.
🐈
A smart cat with an affable
nature.
🐈
Grows to love its owner
dearly.

Musclebound
Glowing orange eyes and
a short, somewhat
snubby nose are
typical features.
These cats are
broad-chested
and muscular,
with large,
round paws.

RED SELF LONGHAIR

This charming cat looks rather like a cuddlesome fur muff, so densely is it covered with a fabulous ginger coat. Perfection in this breed is very hard to come by. Ideally, the cat should show no shading or tabby markings, but the length of the fur is an effective disguise and can create the illusion of a perfectly even colour. To make matters worse, some top-notch breeding cats were lost during the Second World War and so the type was not revived until some years afterwards.

*P*EKE-A-BOO
Occasionally a peke-faced kitten appears in a litter, having a face that is even more squashed than usual. These kittens may have breathing problems as they grow older.

22

CHUBBY CHOPS

The Red Self has an appealing face, with full cheeks and a pert, snubbed, brick-red nose. The large round eyes coordinate with the coppery colour scheme.

CATERISTICS

🐈

A warm and considerate cat that likes company.

🐈

An attractive and homely companion.

🐈

A Red Self show cat is a rarity to treasure.

MARMALADE MAGNIFICENCE

The silky and voluminous fur coat is dense marmalade-orange in colour. The tail is short and fluffy.

ARISTOCRATS
RED TABBY-POINT SIAMESE

The most striking feature of this beautiful cat is its colouring. The coat is white with a tinge of soft apricot on the back, and its point markings are a warm golden-red. Siamese cats with red markings have been recognized as a pedigree since the 1930s, but the current breed was not developed until twenty years later. In its native Siam, now known as Thailand, these exotic creatures have existed for centuries.

FULL OF ENERGY
Siamese cats are out-and-out extroverts, and it is never easy to predict what they will do next!

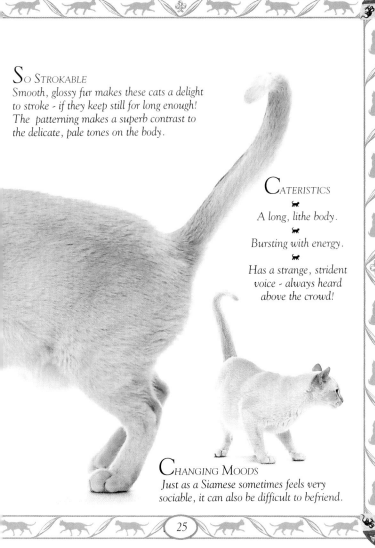

So Strokable

Smooth, glossy fur makes these cats a delight to stroke - if they keep still for long enough! The patterning makes a superb contrast to the delicate, pale tones on the body.

Cateristics

🐱

A long, lithe body.

🐱

Bursting with energy.

🐱

Has a strange, strident voice - always heard above the crowd!

Changing Moods

Just as a Siamese sometimes feels very sociable, it can also be difficult to befriend.

RED CLASSIC TABBY SHORTHAIR

Although looking at first glance a bit like the local ginger alley-cat, there's no mistaking this puss's pedigree breeding: it shows in the superb quality of the coat, with its precisely defined markings - butterfly shape on the shoulders and an oyster-like spiral on each flank - in rich auburn on a background of paler ginger.

DISTINGUISHING FEATURES
The cat's body is sturdy and compact, with large paws, short legs and thick tail. It has a broad, open face, a rose-red nose and paw pads to match.

Copper Cat

Above large, round eyes like shiny copper coins appear markings in the shape of a capital "M". Chest, tail and legs are neatly striped, and there are delicate ginger spots on the tummy.

Cateristics

🐈

Even-tempered and loving.

🐈

Far from stupid.

🐈

Mirror-image markings
on each side.

Wild Design

British Tabby Shorthairs are clever, friendly cats. Their characteristic striped patterning comes close to that of their wild ancestors, whose need for adequate camouflage was, needless to say, absolutely vital for the survival of the fittest.

ALLEY CAT

Wilbur is a delicate- and innocent-looking cat, but a closer look at his left ear will reveal a missing chunk - the result of a particularly vicious fight. His looks are deceptive. When neighbours complained about his backyard brawling and he started to stray widely, his owners felt obliged to have him neutered, but he has calmed down a lot since those early fighting days!

GINGER CREAM
The surprisingly coarse fur, with creamy tabby markings, lightens further on the paws and on the tail, which looks as if it has been dipped in cream!

FIGHTING FORM
Wilbur's build is not unlike the British Shorthair - agile and fairly lean, but resilient and healthy.

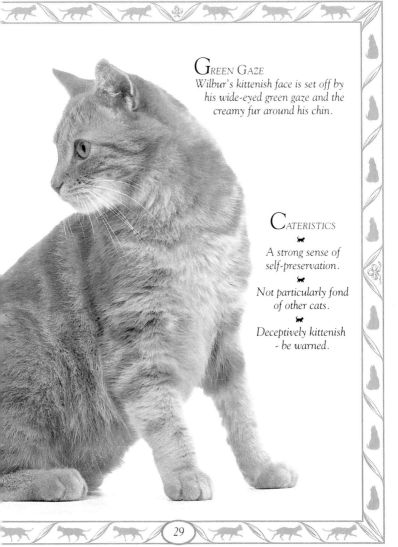

GREEN GAZE

Wilbur's kittenish face is set off by his wide-eyed green gaze and the creamy fur around his chin.

CATERISTICS

A strong sense of self-preservation.

Not particularly fond of other cats.

Deceptively kittenish - be warned.

BRAWLING CAT

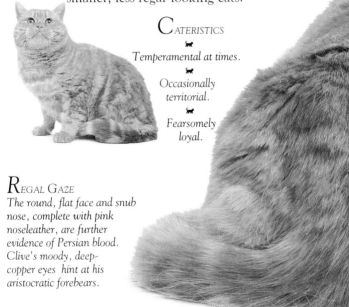

The Persian blood in this large and luscious cat is one of his most striking features. The dense, flowing fur and the distinctly Persian facial characteristics and body type give this splendid cat an imperious air and an outright physical advantage over smaller, less regal-looking cats.

CATERISTICS

🐾

Temperamental at times.

🐾

Occasionally territorial.

🐾

Fearsomely loyal.

REGAL GAZE
The round, flat face and snub nose, complete with pink noseleather, are further evidence of Persian blood. Clive's moody, deep-copper eyes hint at his aristocratic forebears.

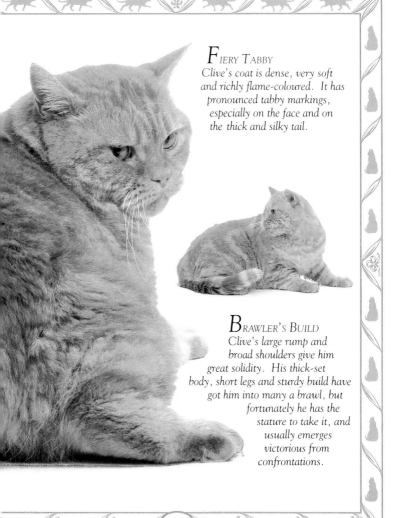

*F*IERY TABBY
Clive's coat is dense, very soft
and richly flame-coloured. It has
pronounced tabby markings,
especially on the face and on
the thick and silky tail.

*B*RAWLER'S BUILD
Clive's large rump and
broad shoulders give him
great solidity. His thick-set
body, short legs and sturdy build have
got him into many a brawl, but
fortunately he has the
stature to take it, and
usually emerges
victorious from
confrontations.

FAMILY CAT

This chubby chappie has just as much charm and style as any pedigree cat - and he could well be stronger and fitter, too. Theory has it that "hybrid" cats, of mixed blood and background, are tougher than the more delicate, pure-bred cats produced for the rarefied atmosphere of the cat show. The non-pedigree version has every ounce as much grace and personality.

TABBY TRACES
The very faintest vestiges of tabby striping appear on the flanks and tail.

Caterstics

🐾

Loving and lovable: the
ideal family cat.

🐾

Resilient and easy to
care for.

🐾

Unique - in markings,
temperament and
characteristics.

Perfect Packaging

The body is sturdy
and strong and the
legs short, but in
proportion. The
coat is short and
soft, kept in perfect
trim by its owner.
The paw pads and
nose are pale pink
in colour.

One-off Design

White socks and bib, plus a white face with random, appealing ginger
blobs on the nose and chin, create an air of individuality and
illustrate beautifully how non-pedigree cats come in a
million-and-one unique and totally
unpredictable packages.

SOPHISTICATED CAT

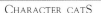

This cat is by no means camera-shy: she has in commercials all over Europe. However, fame, fortune and sophistication have not taken away her marvellous sense of fun: she is inquisitive and especially playful when it comes to unwinding reams of kitchen roll - and her sweet, appealing nature means she nearly always gets away with it.

Amber Eyes

Tizer's features are similar to those of the British Shorthair: a short, blunt nose with a delicate pink nosepad, a well-defined chin and shapely ears. Her eyes are an arresting shade of pale amber.

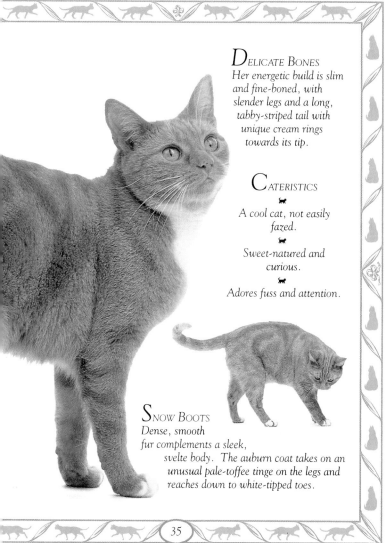

DELICATE BONES
Her energetic build is slim and fine-boned, with slender legs and a long, tabby-striped tail with unique cream rings towards its tip.

CATERISTICS
🐈

A cool cat, not easily fazed.

🐈

Sweet-natured and curious.

🐈

Adores fuss and attention.

SNOW BOOTS
Dense, smooth fur complements a sleek, svelte body. The auburn coat takes on an unusual pale-toffee tinge on the legs and reaches down to white-tipped toes.

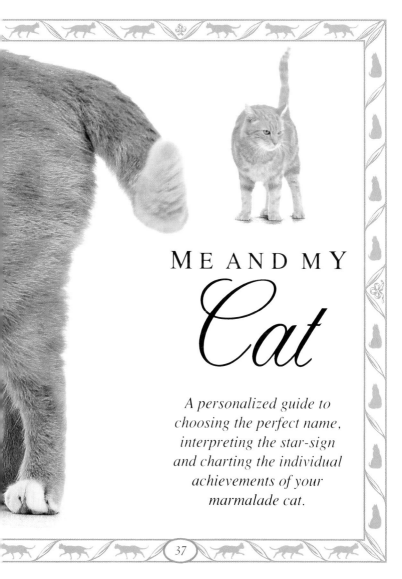

ME AND MY
Cat

*A personalized guide to
choosing the perfect name,
interpreting the star-sign
and charting the individual
achievements of your
marmalade cat.*

MY CAT'S PURR-SONAL HISTORY

My cat's name ..... Sandy

Date of birth ..... Possibly 28 April 1991

Birthplace ..... Mootie's shed (Burravoe) north roe

Weight .....

Star-sign ..... Taurus

Colour of eyes ..... Amber

Colour of coat ..... Sandy

Distinguishing features ..... Stripes and long tail

Mother and father (if known) ..... white cat (mother) Red cat stays at the croftgreen, back of ness, Burrou

Brothers and sisters ..... Kiki, smudy, toby, rest in the loch.

MY CAT'S FAVOURITE THINGS

Gastronomic goodies ..... Turkey, boiled fish, smoked fish,

Snoozing spots ..... chair, side of units, sheepskin mat.

Cat-tricks and games ..... playing with toy horse.

Special stroking zones ..... nose & chin & belly

Main scratching post ..... corner at the hoover.

THE FIRST TIME MY CAT...

Opened its eyes ...... *9 days old.* ......

Drank a saucer of milk ......

Ate solid food ......

Sat on my lap and purred ......

Said "Miaow!" properly ......

Went exploring out-of-doors ......

Presented its first mouse-gift ......

Got stuck in a tree ......

Tumbled into the bath ......

Met a strange cat ......

Fell in love ......

Ran up the curtains ......

Went missing ...... *Got shut in Andy's garage for 1 night*

Returned home battle-scarred ......

Used body language ......

Used the cat-flap ......

Understood the point of the cat-litter ......

NAMES AND NAMING

"The Naming of Cats is a difficult matter," wrote
T. S. Eliot in *Old Possum's Book of Practical Cats*. He
didn't make it any easier by suggesting that cats should
have "three different names": one "the family use daily",
one that's "more dignified", and one known only to the
cat, a "deep and inscrutable singular Name". Nevertheless,
the following suggestions may solve the problem for you!

AMBER *A translucent resin used to make jewellery. It comes in all
shades of yellow, from deep coppery brown to pale golden yellow.*

APRICOT *Sweet and luscious fruit that is at its best grown against a
sunny wall. A great name for a cat that loves snoozing in the sunshine.*

ASIA *Original home of the first marmalade cats. Great numbers of them
are still to be found living there.*

BUTTERSCOTCH *A sweet, yellowy-brown toffee.*

CADMIUM *An orange pigment used to make paint.*

DUNDEE *A Scottish town celebrated for its fine marmalade.*

GINGERSNAP *A sweet and spicy biscuit.*

GINGILI *The oil that comes from
crushed sesame seeds.*

KALLICRATES *A fluffy marmalade
cat in W. L. George's book entitled* Blind Alley.

MACAVITY *T. S. Eliot's "master criminal", a marmalade cat, very tall and lean, who sleeps with one eye open!*

MARIGOLD *A homely cottage-garden flower of cheery orange.*

PENNY *After the old-fashioned, dark, copper-coloured coins.*

QUEENIE *In memory of Elizabeth I, the red-haired monarch.*

ROGERS *A name for a fleet-footed, nimble cat, after Fred Astaire's dancing partner, Ginger Rogers.*

SAFFRON *The dried stamens of crocus, of vivid, dark yellow, used to add flavour and intense colour to food.*

CAT STARS

Check out your cat's star-sign and pick a compatible pet.

ARIES
21 MARCH - 20 APRIL

Adventurous creatures, Aries cats are not restful pets. Although fiercely independent, they have a very loyal streak, and adore being fussed over when in the right mood. *LIBRAN owners lavish attention on the egocentric Aries cat; AQUARIAN owners like the Aries cat's straightforward approach to life.*

TAURUS
21 APRIL - 21 MAY

The Taurean puss is always purring and is happiest when asleep on its favourite bed. Taureans love food and, not surprisingly, tend to be rather plump.

Placid and easy-going, they react fiercely if angered. *VIRGOAN owners create the home Taurean cats love; PISCEAN owners are relaxed by Taurean cats.*

GEMINI
22 MAY - 21 JUNE

An out-and-about cat that gets restless if expected to be a constant, lap-loving companion. An incurable flirt, the Gemini cat's lively nature makes for fascinating, sometimes exasperating, company. *SAGITTARIAN owners share the Gemini cat's need for challenge; VIRGOAN owners won't restrict Gemini cats.*

Cancer
22 June - 22 July

Ideal for someone who spends a lot of time at home, the Cancer cat will be constantly at your side, climbing on to your lap at every opportunity. But tread carefully: Cancer cats are easily offended. CAPRICORN *owners suit the Cancer cat's desire for stability;* TAUREAN *owners give Cancer cats security.*

Leo
23 July - 23 August

King or queen of the household, Leo cats must rule the roost unchallenged. They have a striking appearance and keep their coats in trim. They adore praise and will go out of their way to attract attention. CANCER *owners like Leo cats taking charge;* ARIAN *owners enjoy the Leo cat's acrobatics.*

Virgo
24 August - 22 September

"Take no risks" is this cat's motto. Intelligent thinkers, Virgoan cats don't mind if their owner is out all day and love a change of scene or a trip in the cat basket. SCORPIO *owners complement the Virgoan cat's enquiring nature;* GEMINI *owners have an independence Virgoan cats respect and encourage.*

*L*IBRA
23 SEPTEMBER - 23 OCTOBER

You can't cosset this sensuous feline too much.
Librans crave attention, are quick to take offence
and don't take kindly to being unceremoniously
shooed off a comfy chair. *ARIAN owners are good foils
for tranquil Libran cats; CAPRICORN owners make the
Libran cat feel snug and secure.*

*S*CORPIO
24 OCTOBER - 22 NOVEMBER

Passionate, magical cats with a magnetic presence.
Leaping and bounding with immense *joie de vivre*,
the Scorpio cat doesn't usually make friends easily
but, once won over, will be your trusty ally for life.
    *PISCEAN owners share the Scorpio cat's insight;
TAUREAN owners entice the Scorpio cat back to base.*

*S*AGITTARIUS
23 NOVEMBER - 21 DECEMBER

Freedom-loving rovers, Sagittarian cats lack the
grace of other signs. Their great loves in life are
eating and human company, but too much fuss
makes them impatient. *LEO owners like the
Sagittarian cat's brashness; AQUARIAN owners are
intrigued to see what the Sagittarian cat will do next.*

CAPRICORN
22 DECEMBER - 20 JANUARY

Unruffled and serene, Capricorn cats are rather timid with strangers. They crave affection but may feel inhibited about demanding it. Be sensitive to their needs. *CANCER owners like the settled existence which Capricorn cats love; GEMINI owners offset the Capricorn cat's tendency to get stuck in a rut.*

AQUARIUS
21 JANUARY - 18 FEBRUARY

Unpredictable, decorative and rather aloof, admire your Aquarian cat from a distance. Inquisitive, this cat rarely displays affection for humans, but observes them with interest. *LIBRAN owners understand an Aquarian cat's feelings; SAGITTARIAN wners share the Aquarian cat's unemotional approach.*

PISCES
19 FEBRUARY - 20 MARCH

Home is where the Piscean cat's heart is. The lure of the garden wall holds no attraction for these cats. Attention centres on their owners, who can be assured of a Piscean puss's single-minded devotion. *LEO owners find Piscean cats entertaining; SCORPIO owners have a dreaminess Piscean cats find irresistible.*

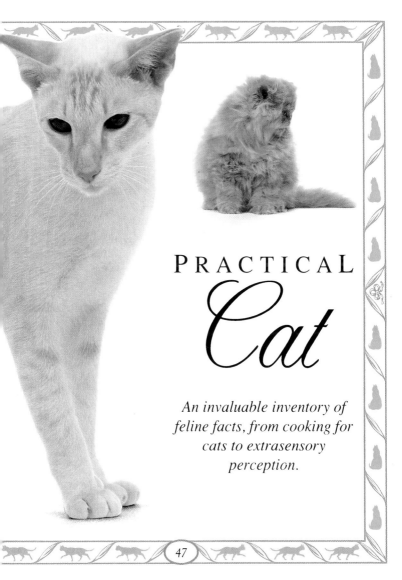

PRACTICAL
Cat

An invaluable inventory of feline facts, from cooking for cats to extrasensory perception.

CHOOSING A KITTEN

Choosing a kitten is great fun - but before your
new friend agrees to move in, she will
want to know the answers to a few questions!

WHICH KITTEN?

Longhairs are luscious, but do you
have time to spend on grooming?
Are you happy to
pamper a
temperamental
pedigree, or
do you want
an easy-
going cat
with an
independent
streak? Should
kitty be prepared
to spend time
alone, and is there
easy access to the
great outdoors?
Does neutering fit
in with your ideals;
if not, can
you cope with
the consequences?

SHOW KITTENS

*At ten weeks, these delightful Red -
point Siamese kittens display all the
promise of fine show cats.*

When you come to choose a
kitten, it is wise to bear the
following pointers in mind:

1 *Choose the brightest, cheekiest
kitten of the litter.*

2 *Look for clear eyes, clean ears
and nose, sound white teeth and
no signs of a tummy upset.*

3 *Make sure the fur is glossy and
healthy, with no fleas, skin
problems or blemishes.*

4 *Check that your kitten is lively
and inquisitive, running and
jumping with ease, eager to play.*

5 *Don't take kitty home under
ten weeks old.*

6 *Check that necessary
vaccinations have been given.*

Homecoming

Bring your kitten home in a sturdy
box. Give her lots of love, play
with her, and don't rush her if
she's shy at first. She'll need a
warm bed, a litter tray that's
regularly cleaned, and her own
bowls for food and water. Let her
have a good look round before she
meets any other household pets.
Keep her indoors for at least a
week. It may take her
a while to feel at home,
but you will know she
has decided to stay when
she leaps on to
your lap with a
contented purr!

CAT-CHAT

Cats are consummate communicators. They use every part of the body, with subtle vocal variations, to make themselves understood. Here is a guide to demystifying feline bodytalk.

TAIL TALK
- A straight tail with a slight kink at the tip means, "This looks most interesting."
- A tail held stiffly at right-angles to the body means, "Hello. How nice to see you."
- A tail with a tip that twitches means, "I'm starting to get angry!"
- A tail waved vigorously from side to side means, "You're for it!"
- An arched tail with the fur fluffed means, "This is my territory and don't you forget it!"
- A tail held low with fur fluffed out means, "I'm frightened." The cat will crouch down and the fur will stand out all over his body.

TONES OF VOICE
- Purring can mean, "Mmmmm, that feels wonderful," or "You're my favourite person." However, cats have been known to purr when in pain or distress, so it does not always indicate contentment.

- A little chirping sound, which mother cats use to marshal their kittens together, is given by adult cats to say "Hi" to their owners.
- A subdued clicking sound means your cat has spotted a bird and is thinking, "Hmmmm, there's my lunch."
- Hissing and spitting mean, "Get off my patch of ground, or else." These noises may have originated with wild cats imitating the sound of an angry snake.

BODY LANGUAGE
- Rubbing the body or head against an object is a way of marking territory. When kitty rubs lovingly round your legs, she is saying, "You're mine."
- A cat with his ears back flat on to his head is saying, "Help!"

• Most owners recognize the pretty little feline hop, both paws lifted together, which means, "Hello, dear friend."

• The cat who greets you by rolling lazily over on to his back, presenting his furry underside for you to admire, is saying, "I feel completely safe with you." Don't be tempted to tickle that fluffy tummy, though: most cats find the area very sensitive, and may react with a reproving paw-swipe.

• An arched back, with straight legs, wide, staring eyes and electric-shock tail means, "Back off now, or I'll attack!"

MAGIC MARMALADE MOMENTS
There are no prizes for guessing where these two gorgeous kittens are headed: their tails say more than words could possibly convey.

CELEBRATION CUISINE

Tsar Nicholas I of Russia fed his cat, Vashka, a celebratory concoction of best caviar poached in rich champagne, with finely minced French dormouse, unsalted butter, cream, whipped woodcock's egg and hare's blood. Rather than trouble his servants, Doctor Johnson himself purchased oysters from Billingsgate for his cat, Hodge. It's not necessary to go to *quite* these lengths on those special days when you want to lavish a little more affection on your puss, but here are some gastronomic goodies which will tempt the fussiest feline.

KITTY VOL-AU-VENT

Spoon a dainty, puss-sized portion of cooked chicken and creamy sauce into the pastry case. Top with prawns for extra-special appeal. Full of protein and vitamins.

LIVER AND BACON BONANZA

Top kitty's portion with crumbled cheese and serve warm. Packed with essential vitamins, minerals and proteins, this is a guaranteed gastronomic success.

Puss's Prawn Cocktail

Fresh prawns on delicate slivers of brown bread, thinly spread with butter and diced into feline-sized mouthfuls. Elegant and full of energy-giving goodness.

Drink To Me Only

Not all cats like drinking milk. Make sure there's always an adequate supply of water for your puss. Or try a tempting sip of evaporated milk, or even milky, lukewarm tea.

Mackerel Puss Pate

A dessertspoonful of mackerel pâté on fresh fingers of toast makes an instant treat for the fish-loving feline. Rich in protein and Vitamin A.

Tuna Treat

Tuna, in oil or brine, topped with crumbled cheese and grilled lightly makes a well-balanced, heart-warming feast for your feline.

Rare Treat

Raw steak or mince, fresh from the butcher's and finely chopped, is a special occasional food for your cat. But be careful not to overdo the raw meat content of your cat's diet.

Sweet Puss

Cats can be partial to the occasional segment of tangerine or apple, or even the odd sweet grape. Full of essential, health-giving Vitamin C and dietary fibre.

CAT GLAMOUR

If you are the proud owner of a longhaired cat, it's essential
to give your pet a daily grooming session.
Shorthaired cats are better at
looking after their coats,
so a good brush-and-
comb once or
twice a week is
all they need.

*T*OOTH *C*ARE
*Check the teeth for
tartar build-up and if
necessary clean with a
soft brush and salt water.*

*G*ROOMING *T*HE *F*UR

1 *Rub grooming powder into the
coat. For best results, always
make sure it is evenly distributed.*

2 *Brush the fur upwards, all over
the body, to remove any trace
of tangles and dirt.*

Fur On The Face
This can be brushed gently with a toothbrush, but stay well away from the eye area.

Eyes And Ears
Clean carefully with cotton wool moistened in a weak solution of salt water.

3 Add the finishing touches by brushing the fur vigorously all over the body.

4 Shorthaired cats can be given extra shine by rubbing the coat over with velvet, silk or chamois.

A-Z of Cat Care

A IS FOR ACCIDENT
The law offers no compensation for cats injured - or worse - on the road. Keep your pet off the street if you possibly can.

B IS FOR BASKET
Useful for travelling, but harder to clean than plastic carriers. Line with newspaper. Try not to leave puss inside for too long.

C IS FOR CAT-FLAP
This saves the trouble of letting puss out and in again. Fit at cat's-belly height and make sure it can be locked securely.

D IS FOR DOG
Cats tolerate dogs' presence in the same household and can form lasting canine friendships if they are introduced in early kittenhood.

E IS FOR EXERCISE
Cats that go outdoors keep themselves fit through energetic adventuring. Housebound cats flex their muscles in boisterous play sessions with their owners. A few can even be carefully trained to walk on a cat leash.

F IS FOR FLEA COLLAR
Put one on puss every summer, before he starts scratching. Cats should wear an identity tag on their collar, in case they stray or are injured.

G IS FOR GRASS
Cats love to eat and regurgitate it, along with any hairballs. Indoor cats should be given a pot-grown clump to graze on.

H IS FOR HANDLING
Most cats adore a cuddle, but pick puss up gently and support his whole weight. Don't grab him by the scruff or hold him under the front legs without a steadying hand under his rear.

I IS FOR ILLNESS AND INJECTIONS

Feline Infectious Enteritis and Feline Influenza are the two big - but preventable - dangers. Have your cat vaccinated at around 12 weeks old and remember to arrange booster shots. Reputable catteries will not accept cats for board without certificates showing proof of vaccination.

J IS FOR JACOBSON'S ORGAN

Cats occasionally make a strange "grimacing" facial expression, with the lip curled back, when delicious smells such as catnip waft past. They are making use of Jacobson's Organ, an extremely refined sense of smell which responds delightfully to certain triggers.

K IS FOR KEEPING STILL

Something a cat can do to perfection, but never when you are trying to administer medicine! Liquids or crushed pills can be added to food. Or grasp the cat's head and bend back gently until the mouth opens. Press on each side of the mouth to increase the gap, and pop the medicine on the tongue as far back as you can. Close the mouth until the cat swallows. Check to make sure the medicine really has gone down.

L IS FOR LITTER TRAY

Keep in a quiet place. Make sure it is always clean and neat. If not, puss may perform elsewhere.

M IS FOR MOVING

Keep kitty under lock and key while the move takes place. When you arrive, let him settle in gradually, a room at a time. Paw-buttering does not prevent straying - much safer to keep puss inside until you're sure he has settled down.

N IS FOR NEUTERING

Nasty but necessary. Kittens should be neutered at between four and six months.

O IS FOR OBEDIENCE

Start young, and be persistent. Say "No" firmly, as you pluck puss off the forbidden chair and he'll soon start to co-operate - at least while you're within eyeshot.

P IS FOR POISONOUS PLANTS

Avoid the following: azalea, caladium, dieffenbachia, ivy, laurel, philodendron, poinsettia, solanum capiscastrum, or keep them out of your cat's inquisitive reach.

Q IS FOR QUARANTINE

Holiday romances can have costly consequences, as the holidaymakers who fell for a Portuguese puss found out. The cost of quarantine for six months exceeded £1000!

R IS FOR RODENT

Cats hunt for sport rather than for nourishment, so be sure to feed your cat well if you want the local mouse colony decimated - a ravenous cat lacks the necessary energy and enthusiasm for exhausting pursuits!

S IS FOR SAFETY

Guard open fires; ban cats from the kitchen when ovens and hotplates are on and store sharp knives safely; unplug electrical appliances where cats might chew the flex; keep upstairs windows closed or inaccessible; lock up household poisons and keep the garage closed; beware when using irons; don't leave polythene bags lying around; tidy up tiny objects that could choke.

T IS FOR TOYS

The best are often the simplest: a cork swinging from a string, an empty box to hide in, an old cotton reel, a felt mouse for pouncing practice, a discarded newspaper to stalk.

U IS FOR UNMENTIONABLE HABITS

Unneutered toms create the most pungent of smells when they mark out their territory. Even if your pets are neutered, you may need to discourage local toms from visiting via your cat-flap and leaving their overpowering mark.

V IS FOR VET

If puss has a prolonged stomach upset, seems lethargic, starts sneezing or coughing, looks rheumy-eyed, or shows signs of pain when handled, ignore any protests and whisk him to the vet straight away. Vets can also advise on vaccinations and booster shots.

W IS FOR WORMS

Most cats suffer now and then. Pills are the answer - your vet can advise on this.

X IS FOR XTRA-SENSORY PERCEPTION

Experts argue that cats have no sixth sense, just highly developed hearing and sight. But anyone who has observed a cat's hackles rise in response to something unseen by human eyes will certainly feel less than convinced by such explanations.

Y IS FOR YOUNG CATS AND KITTENS

Enjoy their antics while they are playful babies. All too soon they will become more sedate and self-conscious, and will save their displays of tail-chasing or shadow-stalking for moments when they think you're not looking at them.

Z IS FOR ZOO

Watch out for the African and European Wild Cats, the closest relatives of the average domestic puss. There is a distinct and uncanny resemblance between a tame, snoozing tabby cat and a slumbering tiger: these and other fearsome breeds, like lions and leopards, feature on a more distant branch of the family tree.

INDEX

ACKNOWLEDGEMENTS

PAGE 10 The Acrobats by Louis Wain / The Bridgeman Art Libary.

PAGE 11 Alice in Wonderland, textile design (detail), C.A. Voysey, courtesy of the Board of Trustees of the Victoria and Albert Museum; The Ginger Cat by Gertrude Halsband / The Bridgeman Art Library.

PAGE 12 The Superior Cat / Mary Evans Picture Library.

PAGE 13 In The Conservatory (detail) by Lavinia Hamer / The Bridgeman Art Library; Holed in One by Louis Wain / The Bridgeman Art Library.

PAGE 14 Orange-striped Cat by Peter Brown / The Image Bank.

PAGE 15 Morris The TV Cat by Miguel Rajmil / Rex Features; still from Breakfast At Tiffany's / The Kobal Collection.

PHOTOGRAPHY : Dave King   ILLUSTRATIONS : Susan Robertson, Stephen Lings, Clive Spong